First published 2019

Copyright © Alistair Jones, @RunningMrJones 2019

The moral right of the author has been asserted.

ISBN 978 164669746 5

FOREWORD

Welcome to the world of Running Mr Jones. I am a runner with more enthusiasm than ability,and a creator of motivational rhymes on Twitter and more recently Instagram. This year, 2019, I ran my first London Marathon and was named 'Running Blogger of the Year' at the Running Awards.

My running journey began in the summer of 2016 when a persistent cough led to a chest x-ray, and an observant consultant ignoring the healthy lungs and spotting the ailing heart. I can't remember everything he said to me as I sat in his office a few days later, but phrases like "lifestyle changes", "need to lose 15 kilos" and "start immediately" thankfully registered. The next day, me and my dodgy ticker started running. Running very slowly at first, entirely recreationally, but with immediate benefits.

The first benefit I noticed from running was a sense of calm. My legs would ache, my breathing would be ragged, I would be hot and sweaty, but my mind would be at peace. This was something beautiful. From the beginning I have found running to be mindful therapy, allowing me to think clearly, beat the blues and bust stress.

Over the next 18 months, my running didn't really improve but my health did. The 15 kilos were lost and I felt healthier and happier. My heart whilst not great, wasn't deteriorating and there were some encouraging signs. By November 2017 though,my running was in a rut. I joined Twitter to connect with other runners and to find a bit of motivation. The running community on Twitter turned out to be a gold mine of encouragement. I immediately felt at home amongst this warm, happy and kind family of runners. In a short space of time I found my voice and much to my surprise, my voice turned out to be poetic.

Having run my first marathon at London, I'm looking forward to running a few more and hopefully one day becoming a six star finisher. Over the next 18 months I will Be Running Berlin, Tokyo, London (again) and New York. As one of my poems says, "running can take you to amazing places and to beautiful faces." I look forward to making lots more running friends and running memories.

So whether you have come for some running with a dash of poetry, or some poems about running, or a just few motivational words to make you smile, I hope you find what you came for. Pour yourself a cup of tea, or a glass of wine, make yourself comfortable, I hope you enjoy the read!

Lainey @_____lainey____

"On my twitter feed you are at the forefront of support and encouragement. Thanks for taking the time to spread your positivity!"

Nina Haglund @5by5Nina

"Some days your encouragement moves me to tears"

Alison Kelvington @Britchick1067

"I really needed this today. Thank you for the encouragement."

John Bloomer @jtbloomer

"Possibly my favourite tweet of all time and me to a tee! #WeeFatRunner"

Caroline Martin @cmartinpsych

"After a few very tricky months, I can actually say I'm back running. I can honestly credit @RunningMrJones for the relentless inspiration and pure kindness getting me there."

Paul Graham @pfgweb

"After a number of years away from running, I started back recently. I'm slow, I'm out of shape, I'm unfit...and have blisters. But reading this I'm inspired and determined."

Liz Ford @FordConsulting

"I've recently completed C25k and missed the structure. I'm so glad I saw your tweet this morning. It got me out of bed, into my running gear and now 5.5km is done. It worked it's magic! Thank you."

Jo @Josopala

"You could have written this for me! Thank you for the constant encouragement, you are now a big part of why I love running"

With my Gold Award for Best Blog at the 2019 Running Awards And some of the lovely feedback for my Twitter blog

DEDICATION

This book is dedicated
To my dearest friend Ken Charlton
who finished his race too soon

With love and thanks
To my parents
Pearl and Reinhard

To my loving family
Monique, Charlie, Jacques and Luis
Juliet, Laura, Lucy, Ethan, Evie and Ollie

To my amazing running partners and true friends
Pete Mack and Phil Askew

To my TeamSpinal family
who made my London Marathon dream come true
Claire Todd, Robin Plowman and Danni Houliston

To Lynsey Hackett of L29 Creative,
who designed the cover and helped create the layout.

To my friend and business partner
Rav Billan for believing in me, encouraging me every
step of the way and advising me on how to turn
my ideas from concepts into a reality.
This wouldn't have happened without you.

DON'T COMPARE
YOURSELF TO OTHERS
JUST RUN YOUR OWN RACE
THERE IS NO SPECIAL DISTANCE

OR ANY QUALIFYING PACE

DON'T LOOK DOWN
ON YOUR RUNNING
OR TELL ME YOU'RE NO GOOD

YOUR BEST
WILL ALWAYS BE ENOUGH
BE PROUD OF IT
YOU SHOULD

IF YOU RUN

YOU ARE AMAZING
DON'T BE TOLD OTHERWISE!

♥@RunningMrJones

SET YOUR OWN GOALS
FIND YOUR OWN PACE
RUN HOW FAR YOU WANT TO

MAKE IT YOUR OWN RACE
RUN ALONE IF YOU CHOOSE
OR JOIN UP WITH A FRIEND
WEAR A SMILE AT THE START
KEEP SMILING TO THE END
COMPETE IF YOU WANT TO
COMPLETE IF YOU CAN

JUST RUN IT IN SUCH A WAY
THAT YOU'LL BE GLAD YOU RAN!

SOMETIMES WE NEED TO **THINK** LESS AND DO MORE IT'S SO EASY TO TALK YOURSELF **OUT OF A RUN**

MY MIND IS
CLEARER
MY HEART IS
STRONGER
MY SLEEP IS
DEEPER
MY WEIGHT IS
DECREASING
MY HEALTH IS
IMPROVED
I CONCENTRATE
BETTER
I HAVE NEW
FRIENDS
I WORRY LESS AND
SMILE MORE
AND YET STILL
I'M ASKED:
WHY DO YOU
LIKE RUNNING?

WOULD YOU LIKE TO

WAVE GOODBYE TO A
LITTLE STRESS
LOSE A
LITTLE WEIGHT
HAVE A HEALTHY
LITTLE HEART
AND PUT A
LITTLE SMILE
ON YOUR FACE?
LET'S START TODAY
LET'S GO RUNNING
WE CAN START WITH
A LITTLE ONE!

RUNNING ISN'T A VIDEO GAME
DON'T ALWAYS CHASE
A NEW HIGH SCORE
SOMETIMES WE SHOULD RUN
TO LET GO OF STRESS
ENJOY THE COMPANY
OF FRIENDS
SEE THE BEAUTY
AROUND YOU
FILL YOUR LUNGS WITH
FRESH AIR
FILL YOUR SOUL
WITH GOOD CHEER
IF YOU FOCUS ON NUMBERS
YOU CAN MISS THE
BEST BITS

YOU MAY NOT BE FAST
YOU MAY NOT RUN FAR
BUT YOU RAN
FURTHER AND FASTER
THAN EVERYONE WHO
STAYED IN BED
OR SAT ON THE SOFA
WATCHING TV

RUNNERS CARE

THEY CARE ABOUT

THEMSELVES
THEIR BODIES
THEIR MENTAL HEALTH
THEIR FITNESS
THEY CARE ABOUT

EACH OTHER

THEY ENCOURAGE

THEY SUPPORT

THEY CONGRATULATE

THEY CARE ABOUT OTHERS
RAISING MILLIONS FOR

CHARITY

PROUD TO BE PART
OF THIS WONDERFUL CARING

RUNNING COMMUNITY

THE JOY OF
RUNNING
IS YOU CHOOSE

YOU CHOOSE
THE WHEN
AND THE WHERE
THE QUICK
THE SLOW
THE NEAR
THE FAR
THE FUN

THE CHALLENGE
IT'S ALL AS
INDIVIDUAL
AS YOU

THERE ARE TIMES
WHEN I THINK I CAN'T RUN
ANOTHER STEP
WHEN I WANT TO GIVE UP

YET OFTEN I REALISE
IT'S MY MIND THAT'S TIRED
NOT MY BODY
AS RUNNERS WE NEED

PLENTY OF SELF BELIEF

AND MENTAL TOUGHNESS
**BECAUSE
THE BODY**
WILL DO WHAT
**THE MIND
TELLS IT**
DON'T GIVE UP TOO SOON

#KEEPRUNNING

WHY DO I RUN?
I WORRY LESS
MY HEART BEATS STRONGER
MY WEIGHT IS DOWN
MY DEEP SLEEP'S LONGER
I'VE MADE NEW FRIENDS
SEEN LOVELY PLACES
ON TRAINING RUNS
AND JOINING RACES
MY MOOD IMPROVES
WHEN I RUN
I'VE SURPRISED MYSELF
BY THINGS I'VE DONE!
THIS IS WHY I RUN ...
WHY DO YOU RUN?

RUNNERS BEWARE:
REGULAR RUNNING
CAN PRODUCE
THE FOLLOWING
DANGEROUS SYMPTOMS
FEELINGS OF WELLBEING

INCREASED STAMINA
SENSE OF PURPOSE

IMPROVED SELF CONFIDENCE
RELIEF OF STRESS

UNEXPECTED FRIENDSHIPS
HEALTHY HEART AND MIND

WHY RISK IT?
STAY SAFE, BE SAD, DON'T RUN

MAYBE YOU RUN TO
BE FITTER
OR SLIMMER
MAYBE YOU RUN TO FIND
PEACE OF MIND
MAYBE YOU RUN TO
EAT CAKE
OR DRINK GIN
MAYBE YOU RUN TO
WIN NICE
SHINY BLING
MAYBE YOU RUN
TO ESCAPE
FROM PROBLEMS
YOUR PAST
THE NOISE
IN YOUR HEAD
WE ALL HAVE REASONS
FOR RUNNING
AND RUNNING
ALWAYS HELPS

TO BE A GREAT
RUNNER
HERE'S A SURPRISE
THERE'S NO
SPECIAL SHAPE
NO PARTICULAR SIZE
YOU DON'T HAVE TO
BE SPEEDY
OR RUN OH SO FAR
IN FACT YOU'LL BE
PERFECT
JUST AS YOU ARE
THE SECRET OF
RUNNING
AS YOU PULL ON YOUR VEST
IS TO RELAX
AND ENJOY IT
JUST GIVE IT
YOUR BEST

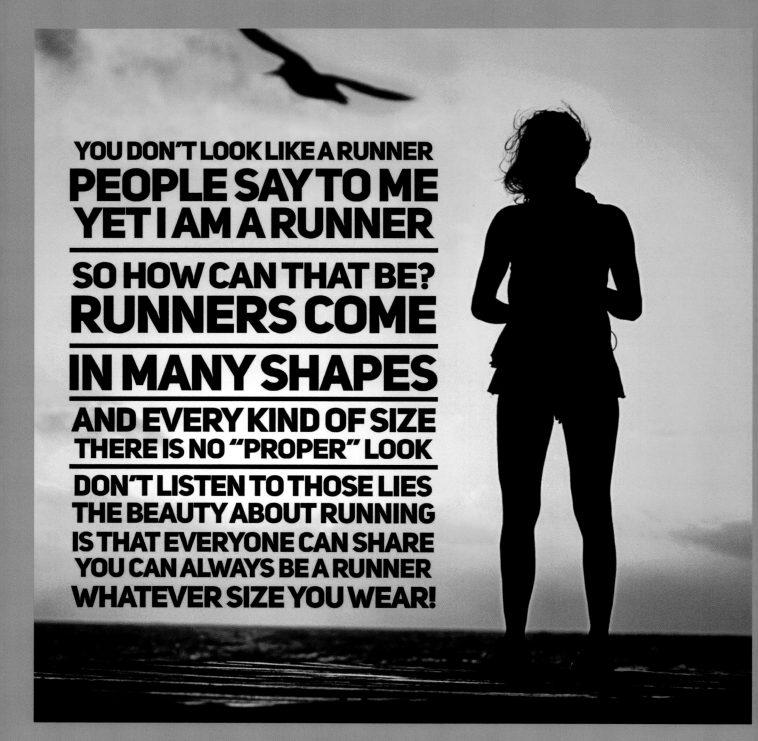

YOU DON'T LOOK LIKE A RUNNER
PEOPLE SAY TO ME
YET I AM A RUNNER

SO HOW CAN THAT BE?
RUNNERS COME

IN MANY SHAPES
AND EVERY KIND OF SIZE
THERE IS NO "PROPER" LOOK

DON'T LISTEN TO THOSE LIES
THE BEAUTY ABOUT RUNNING
IS THAT EVERYONE CAN SHARE
YOU CAN ALWAYS BE A RUNNER
WHATEVER SIZE YOU WEAR!

ARE YOU OFTEN
FULL OF DOUBT?
DO YOU STRUGGLE
TO GET OUT?
PLEASE DON'T WORRY
IT'S NOT JUST YOU
OTHER RUNNERS
FEEL IT TOO
TIME IS TIGHT AND
LIFE IS TOUGH
AT TIMES WE ALL
HAVE HAD ENOUGH
BUT IF YOU CAN RUN
PEACE YOU'LL FIND
TO WARM YOUR HEART
AND EASE YOUR MIND!

#RUNNINGHELPS

WHEN YOU LOSE YOUR
RUNNING MOJO
WHAT ARE YOU SUPPOSED TO DO?
MAYBE ONE OF THESE SUGGESTIONS
**MIGHT PROVE TO BE
THE KEY FOR YOU
PERSUADE A FRIEND**

TO COME AND JOIN YOU
MAKE A PLAYLIST FOR YOUR RUN
VARY UP THE ROUTES YOU TAKE
SET SOME GOALS BUT

MAKE IT FUN

MY PLAN SAYS RUN
MY MIND SAYS NO
I KNOW I REALLY
OUGHT TO GO

I'M FEELING WEARY
FULL OF DOUBTS
THE STRUGGLE'S REAL
TO GET OUT

IF YOU FEEL THIS WAY
DON'T LOSE HEART
IT'LL COME TOGETHER
WHEN YOU START
PUT YOUR KIT ON

GET OUT THE DOOR
YOU'LL QUICKLY FEEL
YOUR SPIRITS SOAR

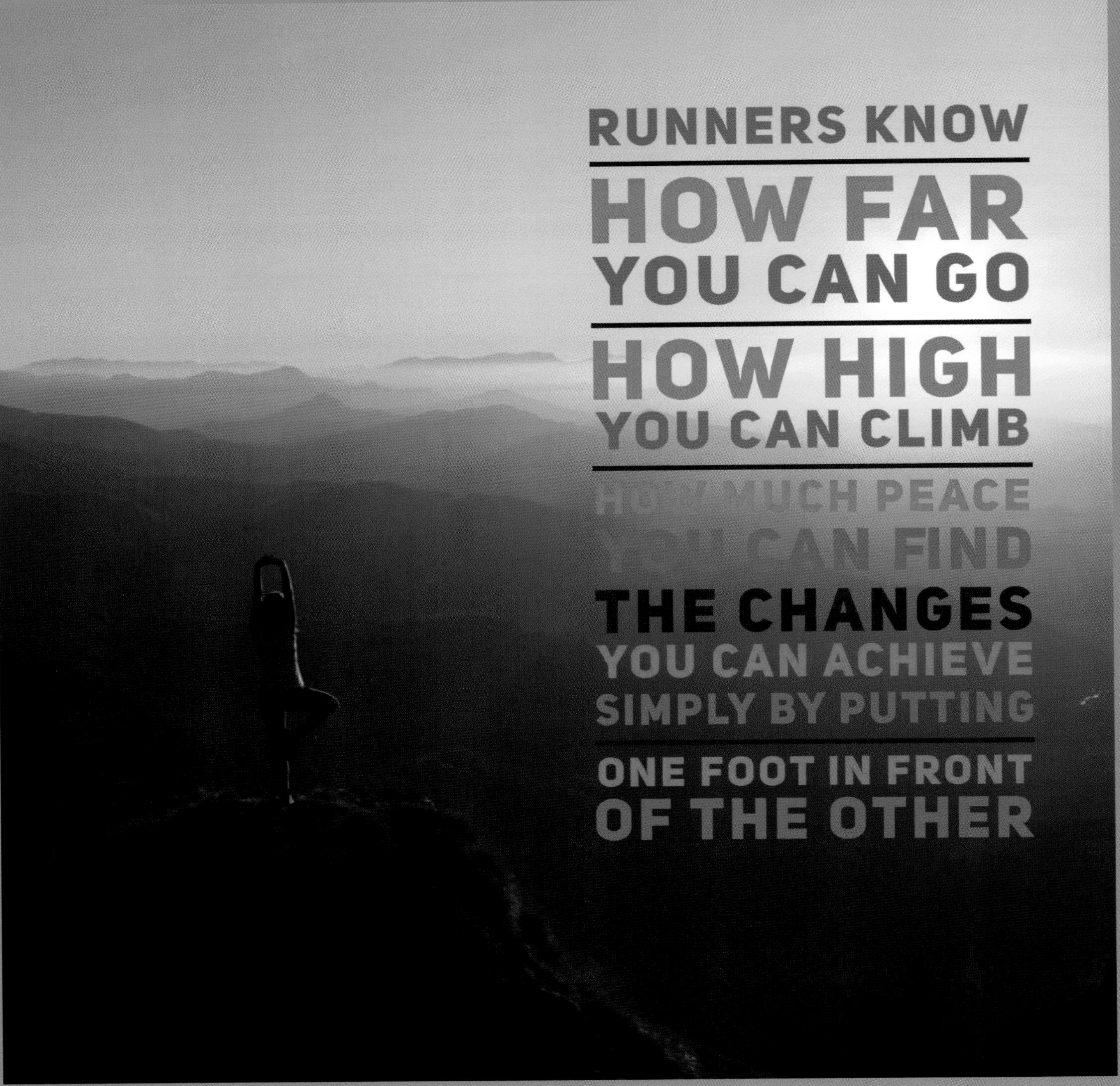

RUNNERS KNOW

HOW FAR
YOU CAN GO

HOW HIGH
YOU CAN CLIMB

HOW MUCH PEACE
YOU CAN FIND

THE CHANGES
YOU CAN ACHIEVE
SIMPLY BY PUTTING

ONE FOOT IN FRONT
OF THE OTHER

SOME OF US RUN
FOR FITNESS
SOME OF US RUN
FOR PEACE OF MIND
SOME OF US
RUN FOR CAKE
SOME OF US
RUN FOR MEDALS
SOME OF US RUN
TO BE A BETTER ME

AND SOME OF US
ARE RUNNING AWAY
FROM OUR PAST
OUR PROBLEMS
THE MADNESS OF LIVING
WE RUN FOR
DIFFERENT REASONS
BUT RUNNING
ALWAYS HELPS

THIS MORNING
I RAN
BECAUSE I HAD TO
I KNOW YOU WILL
UNDERSTAND

WHAT I LOVE ABOUT RUNNING
IS THAT IT'S OPEN TO ALL
IF YOU'RE SPEEDY OR SNAIL
PLUS SIZED OR SMALL
THERE'S NO SPECIAL TEST
NO SUBS TO PAY
IF YOU WANT TO BE A RUNNER

YOU CAN START STRAIGHT AWAY
THERE'S NO QUALIFYING TIME
OR PACE YOU MUST RUN

JUST LACE UP YOUR TRAINERS
AND JOIN IN THE FUN

I'LL BE A REAL RUNNER
WHEN I CAN RUN
A LITTLE FASTER
I'LL BE A REAL RUNNER
WHEN I CAN RUN
A LITTLE FURTHER
I'LL BE A REAL RUNNER
WHEN I WEIGH
A LITTLE LESS
I'LL BE A REAL RUNNER
WHEN I GET LESS
OUT OF BREATH
NONE OF THIS IS TRUE
YOU ARE A
REAL RUNNER
THE MOMENT YOU
START RUNNING!

TODAY I'LL TRY TO
RUN A LITTLE BIT
FURTHER
TRAIN A LITTLE BIT
HARDER
GO A LITTLE BIT
FASTER
STAND A LITTLE BIT
TALLER

BE A LITTLE BIT
KINDER
EAT A LITTLE BIT
CLEANER
SMILE A LITTLE BIT
WIDER

RUNNING CAN BRING OUT

THE VERY BEST OF YOU!

YOU DON'T HAVE TO
WIN RACES
TO BE A STAR
IN MY SHOW
YOUR PACE ISN'T IMPORTANT

NOR HOW FAR YOU GO

THE RUNNERS I LOVE
RUN WITH REAL PASSION
WEAR AWESOME SMILES
AND QUESTIONABLE FASHION
ARE ALL SHAPES AND SIZES
BUT ONCE IN THEIR VEST
THEY RUN WITH

THEIR HEART

AND GIVE IT
THEIR BEST

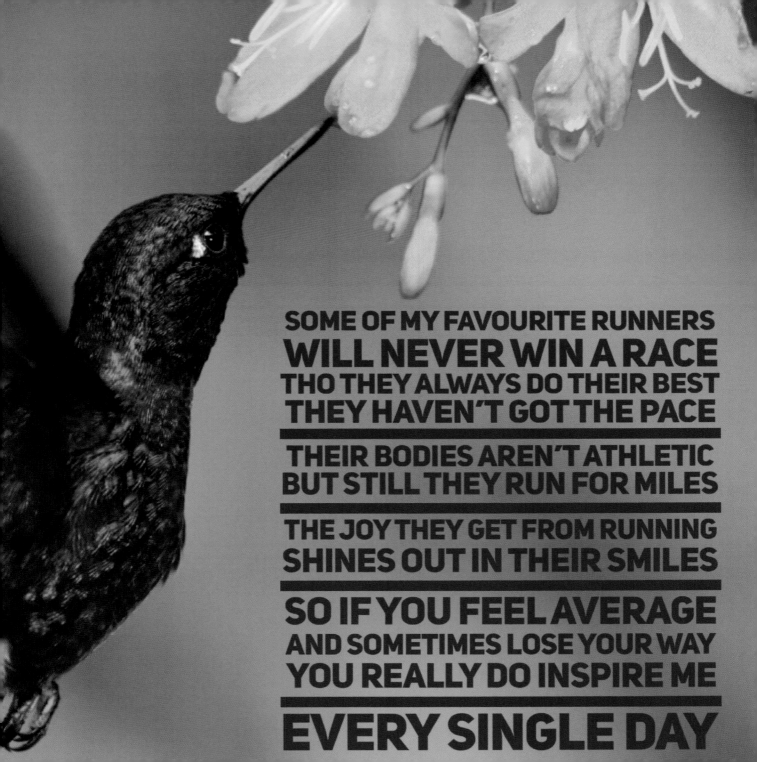

SOME OF MY FAVOURITE RUNNERS
WILL NEVER WIN A RACE
THO THEY ALWAYS DO THEIR BEST
THEY HAVEN'T GOT THE PACE

THEIR BODIES AREN'T ATHLETIC
BUT STILL THEY RUN FOR MILES

THE JOY THEY GET FROM RUNNING
SHINES OUT IN THEIR SMILES

SO IF YOU FEEL AVERAGE
AND SOMETIMES LOSE YOUR WAY
YOU REALLY DO INSPIRE ME

EVERY SINGLE DAY

RUNNING CAN CALM THE STORM
INSIDE MY TROUBLED MIND

RUNNING CAN BRING THE SUNSHINE
TO BANISH MY GREYEST MOODS
RUNNING CAN LIFT ME UP
WHEN PROBLEMS PULL ME DOWN
RUNNING HELPS ME FIND MYSELF

WHEN I'M FEELING LOST.
THE DAYS YOU FEEL
LEAST LIKE RUNNING
ARE THE DAYS
YOU NEED IT MOST!

RUN LIKE THE
SUN IS SHINING
RUN TO THE BEAT
OF YOUR FAVOURITE SONG
RUN WEARING
YOUR BIGGEST SMILE
RUN UNTIL
YOUR HEART
IS POUNDING
RUN UNTIL ALL
YOUR TROUBLES
SEEM SMALL
WHATEVER YOU DO
FIND TIME TO RUN

SOME OF THE
RUNNERS
WHO IMPRESS ME
THE MOST
AREN'T ALWAYS THE
FASTEST
OR FIRST
PAST THE POST
SOME ARE QUITE
CUDDLY
THEIR CONFIDENCE LOW
BUT THEY PULL ON
THEIR TRAINERS
AND GIVE IT A GO
IF YOU QUESTION YOUR
SHAPE
YOUR DISTANCE
OR PACE
YOU'RE MY TYPE
OF RUNNER
THE KIND I
EMBRACE

I'M A SORT OF
RUNNER
BUT I'M NOT
VERY GOOD
I'D LOVE TO RUN
FASTER
IF ONLY I COULD
I'D LIKE TO BE
THINNER
BUT ALSO LOVE CAKE
AND OFTEN AT RACES
I FEEL A BIT FAKE
BUT I KEEP
GETTING OUT THERE
THOUGH I STRUGGLE TO START
GIVING RUNNING
MY BEST
WITH THE WHOLE OF
MY HEART

TODAY I RAN
IN SUNSHINE
FILLING MY LUNGS
WITH FRESH AIR
FEELING THE SUN
KISS MY FACE
IT WAS THE
PERFECT START
TO A BEAUTIFUL DAY
I'VE COME HOME
WITH SUNSHINE
IN MY HEART
IF YOU CAN
RUN TODAY
LET THE SUNSHINE IN
KEEP RUNNING

WHEN IT RAINS
WE GET WET
WHEN THE SUN SHINES
WE GET TAN LINES
WHEN IT'S COLD
WE WEAR LAYERS
WHEN IT'S WINDY
WE GET MESSY HAIR
BUT COME WHAT MAY
WE KEEP RUNNING

BECAUSE RUNNERS ARE
WEATHERPROOF

I HAVE BITS
THAT WOBBLE
AND QUITE A
FAT BEHIND
YET THE MORE
I RUN
AND TRAIN
THIS TRUTH
I START TO FIND
MY LEGS HAVE
MORE POWER
THAN I EVER KNEW
MY HEART
BEATS STRONGER
MY SMILE
IS BACK TOO
AS I'VE RUN
MUCH FURTHER
AND LOST A
POUND OR TWO
MY BODY
ISN'T PERFECT
BUT I GUESS
IT WILL DO

THERE'S A

MAGICAL MOMENT
ON YOUR RUNNING JOURNEY
WHEN YOU REALISE

IT'S NOT ALL ABOUT
YOUR RUNS
YOUR TIMES
YOUR RACES
YOUR DISTANCE
BUT THAT RUNNING IS MORE
ABOUT OUR
COMMUNITY
ONCE YOU FEEL
THIS LOVE
TAKING REAL PLEASURE
IN THE ACHIEVEMENT
OF OTHERS
YOU UNLOCK
SOMETHING SPECIAL

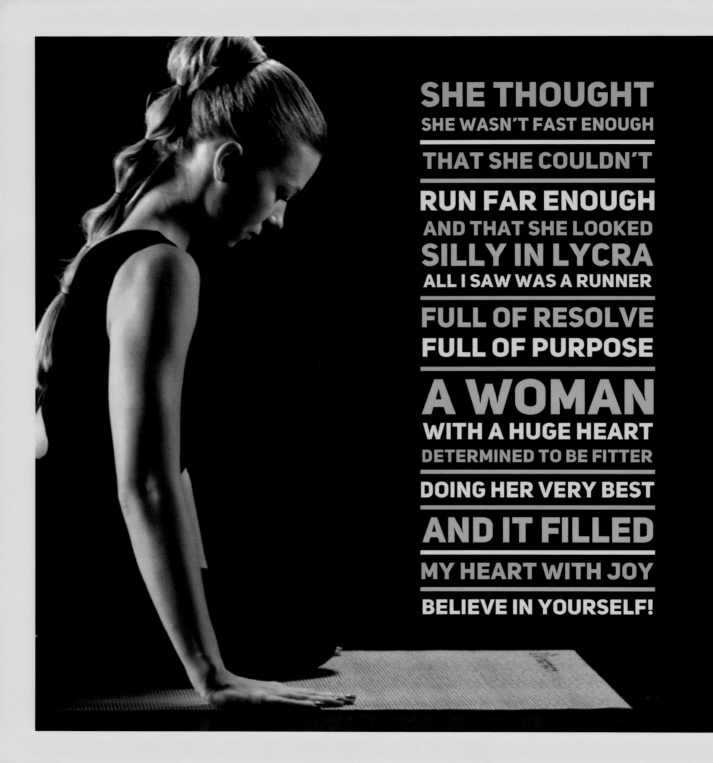

THERE IS SOMETHING **MAGICAL** ABOUT THIS GIFT OF **RUNNING** AND THE MAGIC LIES NOT IN WINNING A RACE OR SETTING A NEW PB **THE MAGIC IS IN THOSE MOMENTS** WHERE YOU REALISE THAT YOU ARE CAPABLE **OF MUCH MORE** THAN YOU THOUGHT YOU ARE IN CONTROL AND THAT BEING ALIVE **IS A TRULY** BEAUTIFUL THING

I LOVE RUNNING

BECAUSE IT SETS MY MIND FREE

CALMS MY ANXIETIES

IT LETS ME EAT CAKE

THERE'S THE GOOD FRIENDS I MAKE

THE FINE SLEEP IT BRINGS

AND SOME OCCASIONAL BLING

MY KIDS ARE INSPIRED

MY SOUL'S LIFTED HIGHER

I'M FITTER AND LIGHTER

MY WHOLE LIFE IS BRIGHTER

WHY DO YOU LOVE RUNNING?

IF YOUR MOJO HAS
UPPED AND GONE
PLEASE DON'T THINK
YOU'RE ON YOUR OWN
WE ALL HAVE TIMES
IT GOES ASKEW
IT REALLY ISN'T ONLY YOU!
BUY SOME KIT
LIST SOME NEW SONGS
GRAB A FRIEND TO TAG ALONG
TRY A NEW ROUTE
OR BOOK A RACE
SOON YOUR MOJO
WILL BE BACK IN PLACE

LONG RUNS
AREN'T JUST ABOUT
THE POWER IN
YOUR LEGS
THEY ALSO REVEAL
THE SIZE OF
YOUR HEART
AND THE STRENGTH
OF YOUR MIND
RUNNING HELPS
ORDINARY PEOPLE
DO EXTRAORDINARY THINGS
KEEP RUNNING
KEEP BUILDING A
BETTER YOU

THERE'S NO QUALIFYING TIME
TO BE A RUNNER
NO HEIGHT RESTRICTION
OR WEIGHT LIMIT
YOU CAN'T BE TOO OLD
OR THE WRONG SHAPE
THERE'S NO IQ TEST
IT'S NOT A POPULARITY CONTEST
YOU JUST HAVE TO BE
THE SORT WHO GETS OFF THE SOFA
AND TIES THEIR LACES
A PERSON WHO DOES
RATHER THAN TALKS

SOME RUNNERS
ARE VERY LEAN
OTHERS HAVE BIG BONES
WE LOVE VARIED SHAPES
RUNNERS ARE
NOT CLONES
SOME RUN VERY FAR
DO SUCH SPEEDY MILES
OTHERS LIKE IT
SHORT AND SLOW
ALWAYS WITH BIG SMILES
ONE THING WE ALL KNOW
IT HELPS OUR
SELF ESTEEM
THOUGH WE ARE
ALL DIFFERENT
WE RUN ON THE
SAME TEAM

RUNNERS ARE
QUITE CRAZY
SOME RUN WHILE
IT'S STILL DARK
THEY STRIDE ACROSS
MUDDY FIELDS
OR ROUND AND
ROUND THE PARK
THEY CLEARLY HAVE

A SCREW LOOSE
WEARING SHORTS OUT
WHEN IT'S ICY
WITH TALK OF SPLITS
AND FARTLEKS
AND THEIR TRAINERS
ARE SO PRICEY!
BE CRAZY
BE HAPPY
BE FIT
RUN

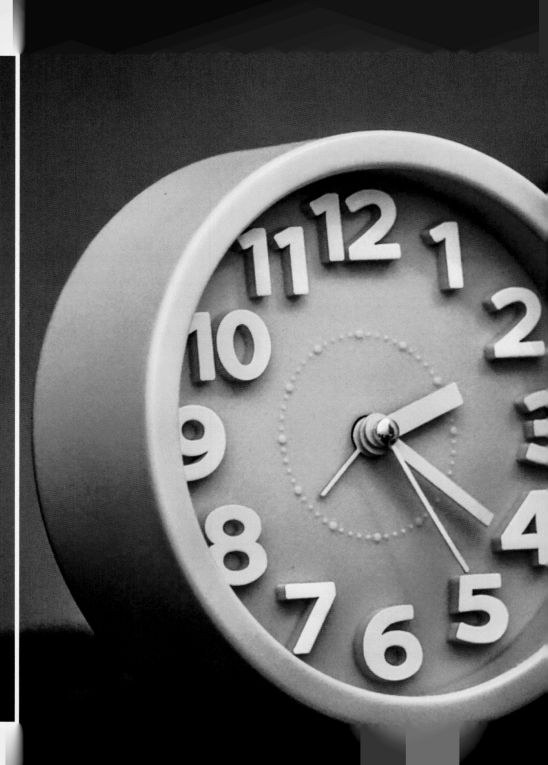

IT'S TIME TO RUN
I KNOW I SHOULD
IF I COULD
GET GOING
I PROBABLY WOULD
BUT I FEEL SO TIRED
MY HEAD'S FULL
OF DOUBT
MY RUNNING MOJO
DOESN'T WANT
TO GO OUT
IF YOU FEEL THIS WAY
PLEASE DON'T
LOSE HEART
REMEMBER IT'S
HARDEST
MAKING A START!
COME ON
TIE THOSE LACES
LET'S GO
RUNNING

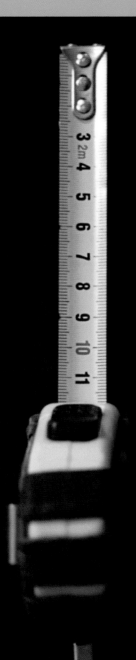

RUNNING MRJONES'
RUNNING RULES
1: DISREGARD RULES
JUST BE YOU
2: RUN HAPPY
3: PUSH YOURSELF
4: SET GOALS
5: REST WITHOUT GUILT
6: VARY THINGS UP
7: IT'S OK TO RUN ALONE
BUT DO ENGAGE WITH
OTHER RUNNERS
8: BE PROUD
OF YOUR ACHIEVEMENTS
9: BE KIND ALWAYS
10: REALLY ENJOY RUNNING

HAVE YOU SAID
I'M TOO CHUBBY
I TIRE OUT QUICKLY
I'M REALLY SHY
I'M TOO OLD
I'M RUBBISH AT SPORT
I'M NOT VERY STRONG
I LOOK SILLY IN LYCRA
I'M NOT CONFIDENT
I'M NO GOOD
AT ANYTHING
NONE OF THESE
THINGS NEED
STOP YOU
RUNNING
START SLOW
STICK AT IT
JUST BE YOU

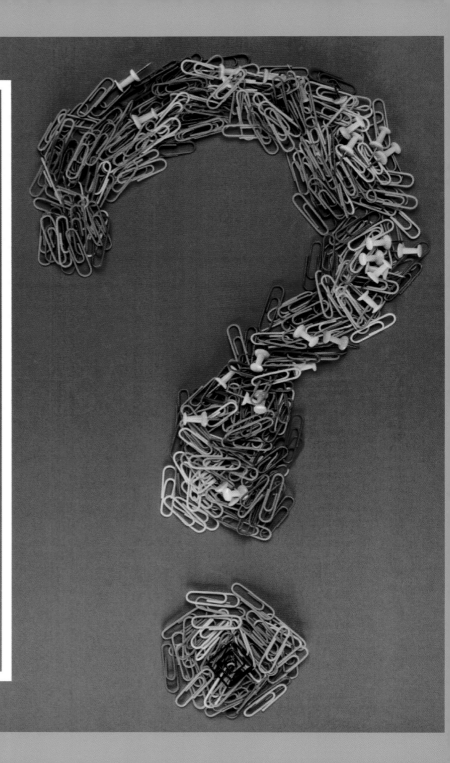

ARE YOU A TINY
BIT CUDDLY
DON'T YOU RUN
EVERY DAY
DO YOU OFTEN HAVE
BAD RUNS
DAYS WHEN YOUR

MOODS ARE GREY

DOUBTING

WHAT YOU'RE DOING
MAYBE FEEL YOU
SHOULD QUIT
YOU'RE NOT MUCH OF
A RUNNER
EVERYONE ELSE IS
MORE FIT
YOU'RE NOT ALONE
MANY AMAZING RUNNERS
HAVE SELF DOUBT
DONT GIVE UP

**MY FAVOURITE
RUNNERS**
THE ONES I LOVE MOST
MAY NOT RUN THE FURTHEST
OR BE FIRST PAST THE POST

MAY NOT BE SO SKINNY
OR RUN SPEEDY MILES
**BUT THEY HAVE
HUGE HEARTS**
AND THE BIGGEST
SMILES
YOU SHOULD FEEL AMAZING
AS YOU WEAR YOUR VEST
NEVER LISTEN
TO THE VOICE
THAT SAYS YOU'RE
SECOND BEST

RUNNING IS FULL
OF LIGHT AND SHADE
AS MY LEGS ACHE
MY SOUL SOARS
AS MY HEART RACES
MY MIND FINDS PEACE

AS MY BREATHING IS RAGGED
MY SPIRIT IS CONTENT
THE PHYSICAL EXERTION
BRINGS A MENTAL CALM
I NEED TO RUN
SO TIE THOSE LACES

BREATHE LIFE
INTO YOUR DAY

WE REALLY DO
LOVE RUNNING
BUT TO GET BETTER

WE NEED MORE
AS WELL AS HAVING
RUNNING LEGS

WE NEED A
STRONGER CORE
A SPIN, A SWIM

A BIKE RIDE
ADD SOME WEIGHTS
INTO YOUR PLAN
IT'LL STRENGTHEN
AND WILL TONE YOU

YOUR RUNNING
WILL BE THE BEST IT CAN
THINK STRONGER

RUN LONGER

RUNNING ISN'T
ALWAYS ABOUT
HOW FAST OR
HOW FAR YOU RAN
SOMETIMES RUNNING
IS ABOUT
HEARING YOUR
FAVOURITE PLAYLIST
FILLING YOUR LUNGS
WITH FRESH AIR
THE CHILDISH DELIGHT
OF BEING
SOAKED TO THE SKIN
IN THE RAIN
OR FEELING SUNSHINE
ON YOUR FACE
RUNNING SHOULD BE
FULL OF JOY

WE COME IN
MANY SHAPES
AND EVERY
DIFFERENT SIZE
SOME OF US
ARE YOUTHFUL
OTHERS ARE
'MORE WISE'
SOME OF US FLY
LIKE THE WIND
WHILST OTHERS
TAKE IT EASY
SOME LIKE TO
WEAR A BAGGY KIT
BUT OTHERS LIKE
IT SQUEEZEY
RUNNING DOESN'T
MAKE CLONES
RUNNING MAKES
INDIVIDUALS
JUST BE YOU!

RUNNING
NOT ONLY STRENGTHENS
YOUR BODY
MAKING YOU
FITTER
LEANER
FASTER
IT ALSO STRENGTHENS

YOUR MIND

IT TEACHES YOU
HOW TO CHASE
YOUR DREAMS
AND TURN THEM
INTO REALITY
KEEPRUNNING

WHATEVER YOU MIGHT
HAVE BEEN TOLD
HOWEVER YOU MAY FEEL
LET ME REASSURE YOU
YOU ARE
GOOD ENOUGH
YOU MOVE
FAST ENOUGH
YOU RUN
FAR ENOUGH
YES, YOU'LL IMPROVE
BUT RIGHT NOW
YOU'RE COMPLETELY
GOOD ENOUGH!
DON'T LET DOUBTS
UNDO ALL YOUR
GOOD WORK
YOU ARE A
RUNNER
SO COME ON
LET'S RUN

I LOVE BEING
A RUNNER
NOT JUST BECAUSE
I LOVE RUNNING
BUT BECAUSE
I LOVE RUNNERS
THEIR BRAVE
KIND HEARTS
THEIR GENEROSITY
TO GOOD CAUSES
HOW THEY ENCOURAGE
EACH OTHER
MY RUNNING JOURNEY
HAS TAKEN ME
TO BEAUTIFUL PLACES
AND BEAUTIFUL FACES
AND FRIENDSHIPS
I'LL CHERISH FOREVER

RUNNING FURTHER
ISN'T JUST ABOUT HAVING
STRONG
POWERFUL LEGS
RUNNING FURTHER
REQUIRES STRENGTH
OF MIND
THE RESOLVE TO IGNORE
THE VOICE SAYING
"GIVE UP!"
RUNNING FURTHER
IS ABOUT HAVING A
HUGE HEART
THAT KEEPS YOU GOING
WHEN YOUR LEGS
WANT TO STOP
TRAIN
BELIEVE
DON'T LOSE HEART

THE BEAUTY OF RUNNING
IS THAT ALL CAN JOIN IN
IT ISN'T RESTRICTED
TO THE YOUNG AND THE THIN
YOU DON'T HAVE TO GO FAR
OR KEEP UP A PACE
IT'S ABOUT TAKING PART
NOT JUST WINNING A RACE
YOU MUST HAVE THE WILLPOWER
TO GET OUT OF THE DOOR
AND TO CARRY ON GOING
WHEN YOUR LEGS SAY "NO MORE"

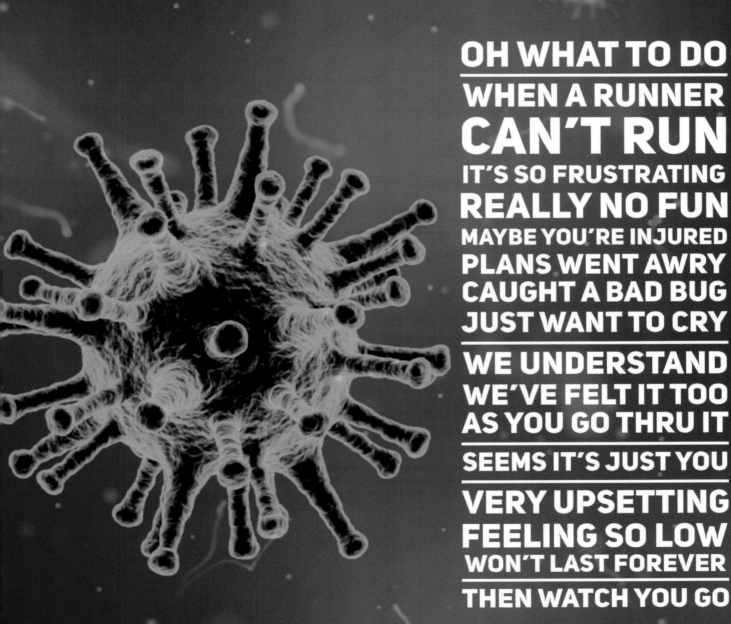

OH WHAT TO DO
WHEN A RUNNER
CAN'T RUN
IT'S SO FRUSTRATING
REALLY NO FUN
MAYBE YOU'RE INJURED
PLANS WENT AWRY
CAUGHT A BAD BUG
JUST WANT TO CRY

WE UNDERSTAND
WE'VE FELT IT TOO
AS YOU GO THRU IT

SEEMS IT'S JUST YOU

VERY UPSETTING
FEELING SO LOW
WON'T LAST FOREVER

THEN WATCH YOU GO

MANY AWESOME RUNNERS
WILL NEVER WIN A RACE
THEY PUT IN EVERY EFFORT
BUT HAVEN'T GOT THE PACE

THEIR BODIES AREN'T ATHLETIC
STILL THEY RUN FOR MILES
THE SIMPLE
JOY OF RUNNING
SHINING IN THEIR SMILES
IF YOU FEEL
AVERAGE
AT TIMES LOSE YOUR WAY
REMEMBER YOU
INSPIRE ME
EVERY SINGLE DAY

SOME DAYS I RUN
LIKE I WAS BORN TO DO THIS
OTHER DAYS IT FEELS
LIKE I'M WADING THROUGH
TREACLE
BUT I'VE LEARNED THAT
IF I GET OUT
AND SHOW UP
LITTLE BY LITTLE
THE IMPROVEMENT COMES
SO IF YOU'VE HAD
A BAD RUN
DON'T GET DOWNHEARTED
IT WAS JUST
A BAD RUN
YOU'RE NOT A
BAD RUNNER

RUNNING
ISN'T ALL ABOUT
BEING FAST
OR RUNNING
CRAZY DISTANCES
RUNNING IS ABOUT
DOING YOUR BEST
HAVING PLENTY OF HEART
IT'S ABOUT GETTING UP
AND GETTING OUT
OF THE DOOR
WHEN IT WOULD BE EASIER

TO STAY WARM INSIDE
RUNNING SHOWS YOU
WHO YOU ARE
AND WHO YOU CAN BE!
DONT STOP RUNNING

MONDAY'S CHILD
IS FAIR OF PACE
TUESDAY'S CHILD
LOVES THE CHASE
WEDNESDAY'S CHILD
HAS GREAT STYLE
THURSDAY'S CHILD
CAN GO FOR MILES
FRIDAY'S CHILD
JUST LOVES THEIR BLING
SATURDAY'S CHILD
HAS A PARKRUN THING
THE CHILD BORN ON
THE DAY OF SUN
DOESN'T WANT TO REST
BUT LOVES TO RUN

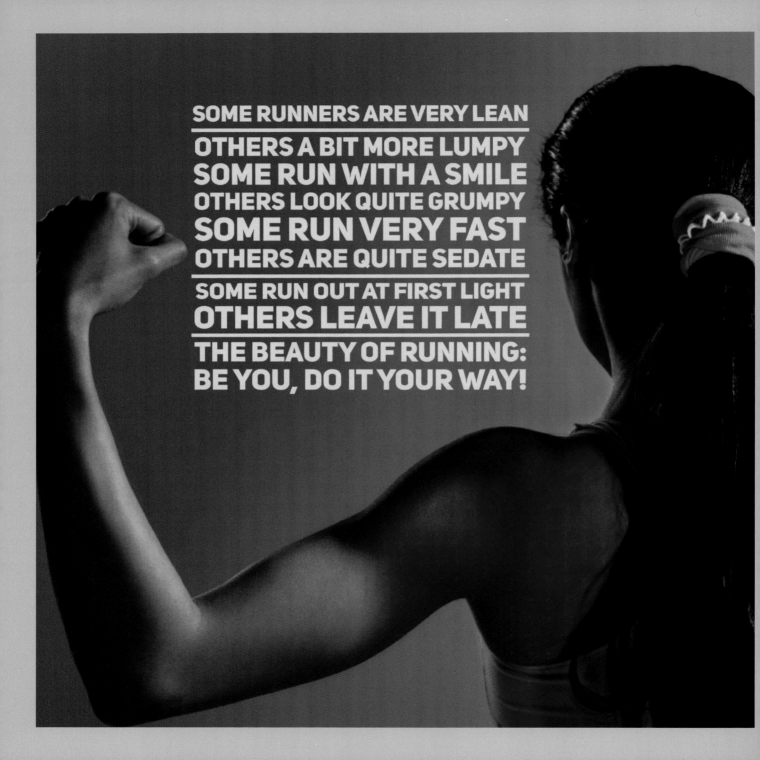

SOME RUNNERS ARE VERY LEAN
OTHERS A BIT MORE LUMPY
SOME RUN WITH A SMILE
OTHERS LOOK QUITE GRUMPY
SOME RUN VERY FAST
OTHERS ARE QUITE SEDATE
SOME RUN OUT AT FIRST LIGHT
OTHERS LEAVE IT LATE
THE BEAUTY OF RUNNING:
BE YOU, DO IT YOUR WAY!

RUNNING TAUGHT ME:
*THE HARDEST PART IS
GETTING STARTED
*GOOD RUNNERS HAVE OFF DAYS
*THE DAYS I LEAST
WANT TO RUN
ARE THE DAYS I
MOST NEED TO
*HARD WORK PAYS OFF
*A BAD RUN IS BETTER
THAN NO RUN
*START EASY, FINISH STRONG
*I CAN EXCEED
MY EXPECTATIONS
*YOUR BEST IS GOOD ENOUGH

SOMETIMES I THINK I HAVE NO TIME **TO RUN TODAY** BUT THE DAYS I RUN I ALWAYS GET MORE DONE **SOMETIMES** I JUST DON'T FEEL **LIKE RUNNING BUT WHEN I RUN** I FEEL SO MUCH BETTER **SOMETIMES** **I THINK I'LL RUN BADLY TODAY WHY BOTHER? BUT GOOD RUNS OFTEN HAPPEN ON BAD DAYS DON'T THINK** YOURSELF OUT OF **YOUR RUN**

LESSONS FROM RUNNING
*THE HARDEST PART
IS GETTING STARTED
*DO MORE, THINK LESS
─────────────────────
*YOU DON'T HAVE TO COME FIRST
TO BE A WINNER
*LOVE THE JOURNEY
NOT JUST THE FINISH LINE
─────────────────────
*IT CAN BE FUN
GETTING SOAKED IN THE RAIN
*EVEN THE BIGGEST HILLS
DON'T LAST FOREVER
─────────────────────
*TAKE IT IN YOUR STRIDE

THERE'S NO WRONG SHAPE
OR WRONG SIZE
YOU CAN'T BE TOO OLD
OR EVEN TOO YOUNG

YOU DON'T GO TOO FAST
OR RUN TOO SLOW
YOU CAN JUST BE YOU
DO IT YOUR WAY
YOU'LL BE PART OF THE TEAM
BECAUSE WE ARE ALL DIFFERENT

BUT WE ARE ALL

RUNNERS

THE BEST COMMUNITY THERE IS

SO MANY EMOTIONS
FROM RUNNERS TODAY

FRUSTRATION AT
CANCELLATIONS
WORRY ABOUT
TRAINING PLANS
BEING A RUNNER
HAS IT'S CHALLENGES
AT TIMES THE WEATHER

OUR BODIES, OUR HEALTH
INTERFERE WITH OUR PLANS

BEING A RUNNER
MEANS WE MEET
THE CHALLENGES
WE GET UP
WHEN WE'RE DOWN
AND RUN AGAIN

PEOPLE JUST DON'T UNDERSTAND
WHY RUNNERS HAVE TO RUN

WHY WE'RE UP AND IN OUR KIT
BEFORE THE RISING SUN
HOW WE FEEL COMPLETELY FREE
AS WE RACK UP MILES
HOW WIND AND RAIN AND EVEN MUD
CAN'T REMOVE OUR SMILES
STAY WEIRD. KEEP RUNNING!

WHEN I STARTED RUNNING

I THOUGHT IT WOULDN'T LAST
I COULDN'T RUN VERY FAR

AND I WASN'T AT ALL FAST
BUT MY WEIGHT WENT DOWN
AND MY FITNESS GREW

MY MOODS IMPROVED
THE GREY SKIES
TURNED BLUE

I MADE GREAT FRIENDS
AND FOUND BETTER SLEEP
REALISED THIS
RUNNING BUG

IS ONE I SHOULD KEEP!

PEOPLE WILL
KNOCK YOU DOWN
PUT YOU DOWN
TELL YOU YOU CAN'T
THAT YOU'RE
NOT GOOD ENOUGH!

RUNNING BUILDS YOU UP
RUNNING SHOWS YOU
HOW STRONG YOU ARE
THAT YOU CAN
THAT YOU ARE
BLOOMING AWESOME
DO NOT GIVE UP!

WHY ARE YOU A RUNNER?
TO IMPROVE FITNESS
TO LOSE SOME POUNDS
BECAUSE I ONCE FELT LOST

BUT NOW I'M FOUND

FOR MY PEACE OF MIND
SOME TIME ALONE
TO FEED MY SOUL
NOW MY JOY HAS GROWN
TO STRETCH MYSELF
AND TO HAVE SOME FUN
TO MAKE NEW FRIENDS
THIS IS WHY I RUN

IT'S A HEARTWARMING
PLEASURE
TO BE A
SOCIAL MEDIA
RUNNER
SURROUNDED BY FRIENDS
WHO LOVE TO RUN
JUST LIKE I DO
YOU CELEBRATE
MY GOOD DAYS
PICK ME UP
WHEN IT'S BAD
YOU INSPIRE ME
WITH YOUR STORIES
HELP ME BE A
BETTER ME
LIFE ISN'T ALWAYS EASY
BUT YOU, MY FRIENDS
MAKE EVERY DAY
BRIGHTER

DON'T COMPARE
YOURSELF TO OTHERS
JUST RUN
YOUR OWN WAY
COMPARISON
CAN STEAL YOUR JOY

LEADING TO DISMAY
MAYBE YOU RUN ULTRAS
OTHERS LIKE A SHORT 5K

YOU RUN ONCE A WEEK

THEY RUNSTREAK
EVERY DAY
IT'S NOT ABOUT DISTANCE

OR EVEN ABOUT PACE
**BUT RUNNING
NEEDS TO PUT
A SMILE**
ON YOUR FACE

SOME DAYS YOUR RUNNING
FEELS SO NATURAL
SOMETIMES YOU CAN'T
FIND YOUR FLOW
SOME DAYS YOU EASE
THROUGH THE MILES
_____

SOMETIMES YOUR
BODY SAYS "NO"
RUNNING CAN BE
QUITE ENIGMATIC
_____

ON THE DAY YOU'RE
FEELING YOUR WORST
THAT'S WHEN YOU
TURN IN YOUR PB
WITH THAT AWESOMELY
_____

FAST SPEEDY BURST

I RUN WITH FRIENDS
YOU RUN ALONE
SHE ALWAYS SMILES
HE LOVES A MOAN
YOU RUN UP HILLS
I LIKE IT FLAT
HE STOMPS ALONG
SHE'S LIKE A CAT
THEY LIKE TO WIN
WE JUST TAKE PART
HE HAS STRONG LEGS
YOU HAVE HUGE HEART
THEY'RE QUITE PLAIN
SHE'S A STUNNER
THO WE'RE DIFFERENT
WE ARE ALL RUNNERS

SHE THOUGHT
SHE WASN'T
GOOD ENOUGH
TOO TIRED
LUMPY AND SLOW
I SAW YOU CONQUER
ALL THOSE DOUBTS

I LOVE TO WATCH
YOU GROW
YOU THINK YOU'RE

ORDINARY
I KNOW THAT'S NOT TRUE
SO MANY ARE INSPIRED
JUST BY WATCHING YOU
YOU CHANGED YOUR WORLD
WHEN YOU FIRST RAN
SHOWED YOURSELF
#THISGIRLCAN

SOME OF MY
FAVOURITE RUNNERS
ARE QUITE
CUDDLY
ARE NOT
VERY FAST
DON'T RUN
SO MANY MILES
SUFFER ANXIETY
WALK UP THE HILLS
STRUGGLE
WITH INJURIES
THEY WON'T GET PICKED
FOR THE
OLYMPICS
BUT I'D HAVE THEM
ON MY TEAM
EVERY
SINGLE
DAY

LIFE ASKS SO MANY
QUESTIONS
IS SO FULL OF STRESS

HAS SO MANY PROBLEMS
MY QUIET TIME
RUNNING
HELPS ME FIND SOME
ANSWERS
A LITTLE RELIEF
AND A FEW SOLUTIONS

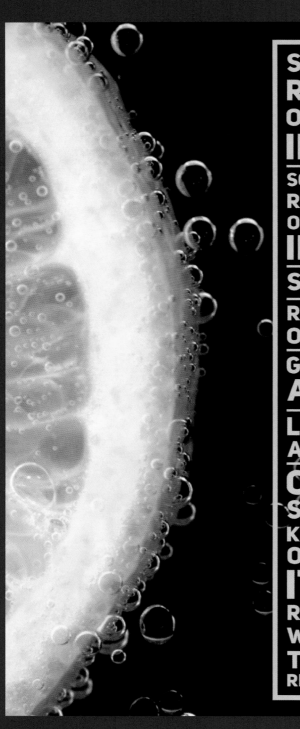
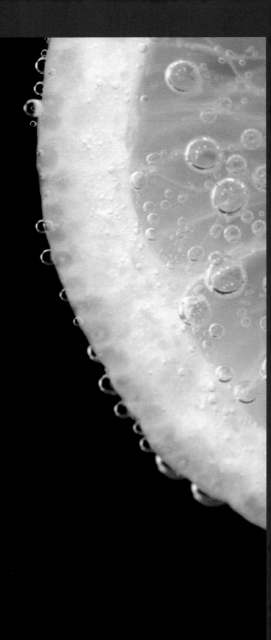

SOME OF US
RUN IN K'S
OTHERS RUN
IN MILES
SOME OF US ARE
REAL SCRUFFS
OTHERS STRIDE
IN STYLE
SOME OF US
RUN FOR CAKE
OR AN EXTRA
GLASS OF GIN
ALL OF US
LIKE TO GET
ANOTHER BIT
OF BLING
SOME OF US
KEEP IT SHORT
OTHERS LIKE
IT LONG
RUN HOW YOU
WANT TO RUN
THERE IS NO
RIGHT OR WRONG

SOME OF MY FAVOURITE
RUNNERS
DON'T LOOK LIKE
RUNNERS AT ALL
MADE A LITTLE BIT
CUDDLY
PROGRESS IS RATHER SMALL
YOU RUN WITH
YOUR HEART
ENCOURAGE OTHERS TOO
SEEING YOU SMILE
I LOVE WHAT YOU DO
THO YOU FEEL
ORDINARY
STRUGGLE TO GET OUT
KNOW YOU INSPIRE ME
YOU'RE WHAT
RUNNING IS ABOUT

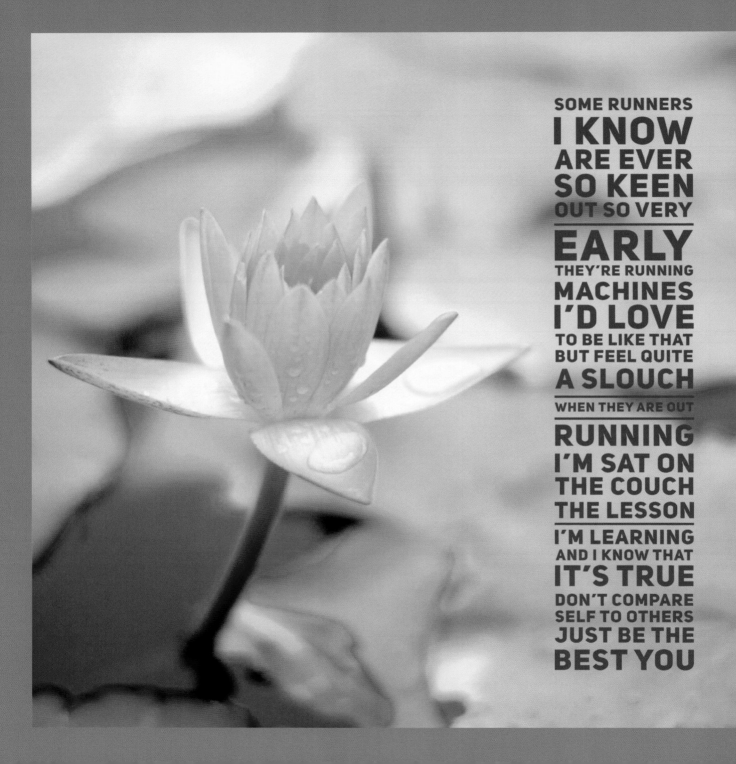

SOME RUNNERS
I KNOW
ARE EVER
SO KEEN
OUT SO VERY
EARLY
THEY'RE RUNNING
MACHINES
I'D LOVE
TO BE LIKE THAT
BUT FEEL QUITE
A SLOUCH
WHEN THEY ARE OUT
RUNNING
I'M SAT ON
THE COUCH
THE LESSON
I'M LEARNING
AND I KNOW THAT
IT'S TRUE
DON'T COMPARE
SELF TO OTHERS
JUST BE THE
BEST YOU

BEING A RUNNER
IS STRANGE
IT CAN HURT
SO MUCH
IT TAKES YOU TO YOUR
MENTAL LIMITS
IT CAN DRAIN YOU OF
ALL ENERGY
YOU SWEAR AS YOU
RUN UPHILL
YOU WONDER
HOW YOU WILL GO ON
AND YET WE ABSOLUTELY
LOVE IT

IF I HAD THE TIME
I'D RUN TOO!
HAVE ANY FRIENDS
SAID THIS TO YOU?
US RUNNERS KNOW
THAT'S NOT RIGHT
WE OFTEN RUN

BEFORE IT'S LIGHT
OR DURING LUNCH
AROUND THE PARK
ROUND OUR STREETS
IN EVENING DARK
THERE'S NO SPARE TIME
IT'S SAD BUT TRUE
YOU MAKE THE TIME
FOR WHAT YOU WANT TO DO!

MY FELLOW RUNNERS
DURING THESE DARK
COLD MORNINGS
WE SHALL CONTINUE
TO RUN
WITHOUT LET UP
WE SHALL RUN
ON THE BEACHES
WE SHALL RUN
AROUND THE PARKS
WE SHALL RUN
IN THE FIELDS
AND IN THE STREETS
WE SHALL RUN
UP ALL THE HILLS
WE SHALL NEVER
SURRENDER

A BRAND
NEW WEEK
LET'S HAVE FUN
MAKE SOME PLANS
TO GO AND RUN
IF IT'S COLD & DARK
THE HARDEST PART
IS TO ESCAPE
THE DUVET
AND MAKE A START
THOSE FIRST
FEW STEPS
ACROSS THE FLOOR
FROM THE SOFA
TO THE FRONT DOOR
BUT YOU CAN DO IT
YES YOU CAN
YOU'LL FEEL
MUCH BETTER
BECAUSE YOU RAN

MONDAY THOUGHT
A NEW WEEK

STRETCHES BEFORE US
WITH NEW MILES TO RUN
NEW DRAGONS TO SLAY
NEW CHALLENGES TO MEET

NEW GOALS TO ACHIEVE
NEW FEARS TO OVERCOME

IT'S OK TO BE APPREHENSIVE
BUT BE ASSURED
YOU CAN DO IT!
SO LET'S LACE UP THOSE TRAINERS

DEAR RUNNERS

I READ ABOUT YOU
GETTING OFF THE COUCH
TO AIM FOR 5K

GETTING ON A PLANE
TO RACE OVERSEAS
RUNNING YOUR 50TH PARKRUN

I SEE YOU SMILING

HOLDING YOUR BLING

OR SOAKED
FROM RUNNING IN THE RAIN

OR COMING BACK
FROM INJURY
EVERY SINGLE ONE OF YOU
INSPIRES ME
THANK YOU!

MY FAVOURITE
RUNNERS
ARE MORE TORTOISE
THAN HARE
THEY CAN BE
QUITE CUDDLY
AND ON HILLS
OFTEN SWEAR
THEY TEND TO
GET ANXIOUS
DON'T RUN ALL THAT FAR
THEY THINK THEY'RE
JUST AVERAGE
BUT TO ME THEY
ARE STARS
DON'T GET
DOWNHEARTED
OR LET YOUR CHIN DROP
YOU ARE A RUNNER
DON'T EVER STOP

RUNNERS

PLEASE STOP TALKING ABOUT

THE FUN OF RUNNING
THE WEIGHT
YOU LOSE

THE PEACE OF MIND
YOU FIND

THE AMAZING COMMUNITY
YOUR IMPROVING FITNESS

AND MENTAL WELL BEING

STOP LOOKING
SO HAPPY
SO HEALTHY

SO CONTENT
IT'S MEANT TO BE OUR
LITTLE SECRET!

IT'S NATURAL TO
FEEL NERVOUS
BEFORE A BIG RACE
WILL I SET OUT TOO FAST
WHAT IS THE RIGHT PACE
SHOULD I AIM FOR A TIME
OR JUST DO MY BEST
DO I RUN A FEW MILES
OR JUST TAPER AND REST
FEELINGS OF MARANOIA
_____

I OVERTHINK EVERYTHING
YOU'RE TRAINED
YOU ARE READY
GO GET THAT BLING

WHEN YOU RUN A
MARATHON
YOU'RE NOT COMPETING

AGAINST THE OTHER

RUNNERS
IT'S NOT EVEN ALL ABOUT

THE CLOCK
YOU'RE RUNNING AGAINST
26.2 MILES
AND AGAINST THAT

**NAGGING VOICE
IN YOUR HEAD**
TELLING YOU TO STOP!

I NEED TO RUN
I REALLY SHOULD
IF I GOT OFF THE SOFA

I SURELY WOULD
BUT I'M SO TIRED
AND DOUBT MYSELF
MY RUNNING MOJO
LEFT ON THE SHELF

IF THIS IS YOU
DON'T LOSE HEART

IT'S OFTEN HARDEST
TO MAKE A START
IF YOU PUSH YOURSELF
TO GET OUT THE DOOR
YOUR RUN WILL LEAVE YOU

WANTING MORE!

I'M SO TIRED

IT MIGHT RAIN
IT'S GETTING LATE
MY MUSCLES ACHE

IT'S SO COLD
I CAN'T BE BOTHERED
I'VE LOST MY MOJO
I NEVER GET BETTER

WE'VE ALL SAID THEM
WE'VE ALL IGNORED THEM
DON'T LET EXCUSES
GET THE BETTER OF YOU!
YOU'RE A RUNNER!
SO TIE YOUR LACES
AND LET'S GO

SOME OF MY
BITS WOBBLE
I'M OFTEN FULL
OF DOUBT
MY RUNS CAN BE
REALLY SLOW
I STRUGGLE
TO GET OUT
MY BREATHING'S
OFTEN RAGGED
MOST PEOPLE OVERTAKE
MY GAIT'S A
LITTLE AWKWARD
AS ARE THE
SOUNDS I MAKE
THOUGH I DON'T
BREAK RECORDS
AND I'LL NEVER
BE ELITE
I'M A REAL
RUNNER
EAT, RUN
SLEEP
REPEAT

PEOPLE ASK ME
WHY I GET UP SO EARLY
TO GO RUNNING

BECAUSE ...

IF I HAD A POUND
EACH TIME A
NON RUNNER
SAID TO ME..
YOU RAN A RACE?
DID YOU WIN?
YOU RAN 10K?

IS THAT FURTHER THAN A MARATHON?
YOU ENJOY RUNNING?
IT'S VERY BAD
FOR YOUR KNEES
ISN'T IT?

WHY ARE RUNNING SHOES
SO EXPENSIVE?
I'D GO RUNNING IF
I HAD THE TIME

I'D BE A MILLIONAIRE

I SEE YOU
PULLING ON YOUR
TRAINERS
FOR THAT FIRST RUN
GOING FROM THE
COUCH TO 5K
STARTING PARKRUN
FINISHING YOUR
FIRST RACE

THE SELFIE WITH BLING
SETTING A PB
STEPPING IT UP TO 10K

RUNNING A HALF

A MARATHON

AN ULTRA
I SEE YOU ALL AND
EVERY SINGLE ONE OF YOU
INSPIRES ME

KEEP RUNNING

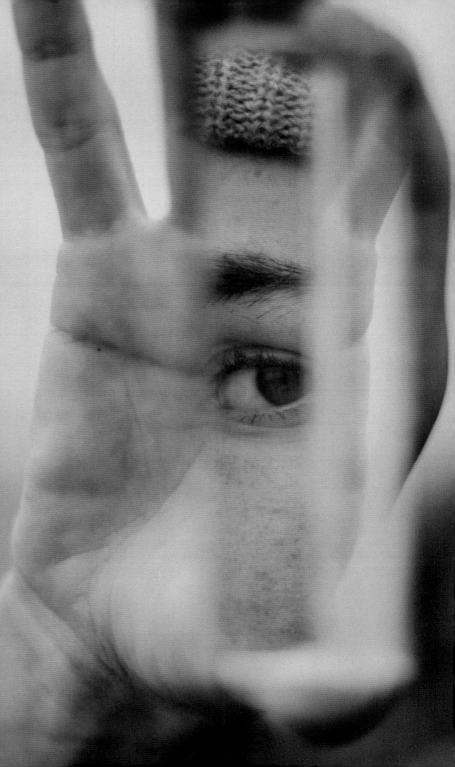

RUNNING
IS LIKE A MIRROR
THAT HELPS YOU SEE

WHO YOU REALLY ARE
AND SOMETIMES YOU
SURPRISE YOURSELF

WHEN YOU SEE
YOU CAME SO FAR
PERHAPS YOU STARTED

ON THE COUCH
NOW YOU RUN
TWENTY SIX POINT TWO
RUNNING SHOWED YOU HAVE

SUCH STRENGTH
SUCH HEART
RUNNING HELPS YOU

FEEL PROUD
OF YOU!

I'M DEFINITELY
NOT LAZY
AND CERTAINLY
NO SLOUCH
BUT THE TOUGHEST PART
OF A RUN
CAN BE GETTING
OFF THE COUCH
THE HARDEST STEPS TO TAKE
ARE THE ONES TO THE
FRONT DOOR
ONCE I GET THOSE DONE
I'M EAGER
FOR LOTS MORE

SO DON'T GET DOWNHEARTED
IF IT'S HARD TO GET STARTED
WE ALL FEEL IT

THE ROAD WE WALK
ISN'T ALWAYS EASY
AT TIMES LIFE
CAN BE TOUGH
SOME DAYS IT FEELS
A REAL STRUGGLE
SOMETIMES YOU'VE JUST

HAD ENOUGH
MANY FIND THAT
RUNNING'S HELPFUL
ON THOSE BLEAK
AND STRESSFUL DAYS

THAT IT CAN BRING

PEACE OF MIND
RESTORE YOUR SOUL
IN MANY WAYS.
#ITSOKNOTTOBEOK

HAVE YOU SAID:
I'M NOT REALLY SPORTY
I'LL NEVER LOSE WEIGHT
I GET TIRED SO QUICKLY
MY STRENGTH ISN'T GREAT
MY AGE IS AGAINST ME
I'M REALLY QUITE SHY
I LOOK SILLY IN LYCRA
SO WHY SHOULD I TRY?
THESE VERY REASONS
ARE WHY YOU SHOULD RUN
YOU'LL FEEL MUCH BETTER
AND HAVE LOADS OF FUN!

WHEN I FEEL LOST

I RUN

AND FIND MYSELF AGAIN
WHEN I'M FULL OF DOUBTS

I RUN

AND BELIEVE AGAIN
WHEN MY HEAD IS
FULL OF KNOTS

I RUN

AND CALM RETURNS AGAIN
RUNNING IS SUCH
GOOD MEDICINE
LET'S TAKE A DOSE

AS I HEAD TO WORK
I SHALL SEE RUNNERS

OUT EARLY, GETTING THEIR MILES
SOME WILL BE BREATHING HARD
RED FACED AND SWEATY
OTHERS TAKING IT EASIER.
I'LL SMILE AT THEM ALL
TRYING TO CONVEY WITH A LOOK
THAT I'M ALSO A RUNNER
EVERY SINGLE ONE

WILL LEAVE ME WISHING
THAT I WAS RUNNING TOO!

DO YOU WANT TO KNOW
THE SECRET
OF BEING A
RUNNER?
YOU JUST
START RUNNING
YOU DON'T HAVE TO
RUN FAR
YOU DON'T HAVE TO
RUN FAST
YOU DON'T NEED
SPECIAL KIT
THERE'S NO FORMS TO FILL
OR SUBSCRIPTION TO PAY
YOU JUST NEED TO
STEP OUTSIDE
THE MINUTE YOU
START RUNNING
YOU'VE BECOME
A RUNNER!

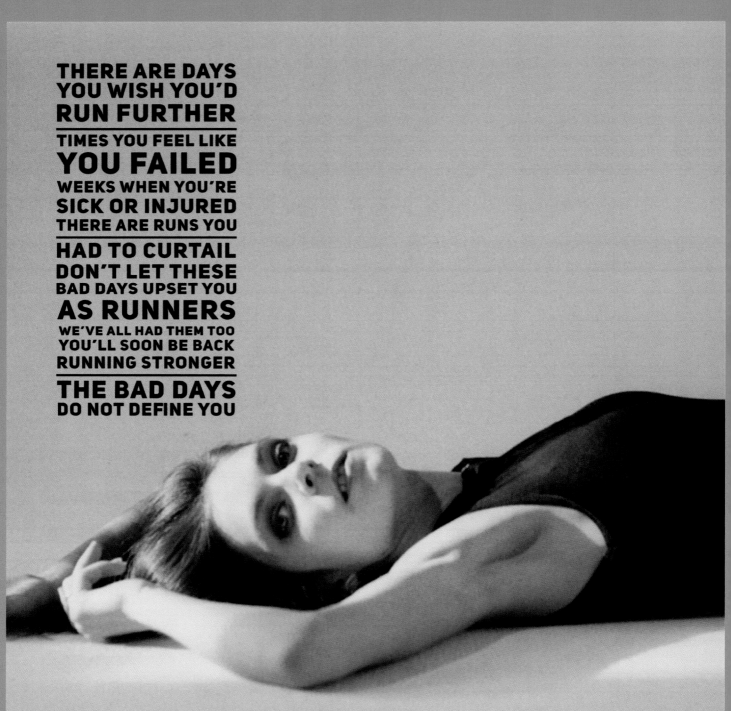

THERE ARE DAYS
YOU WISH YOU'D
RUN FURTHER
TIMES YOU FEEL LIKE
YOU FAILED
WEEKS WHEN YOU'RE
SICK OR INJURED
THERE ARE RUNS YOU
HAD TO CURTAIL
DON'T LET THESE
BAD DAYS UPSET YOU
AS RUNNERS
WE'VE ALL HAD THEM TOO
YOU'LL SOON BE BACK
RUNNING STRONGER
THE BAD DAYS
DO NOT DEFINE YOU

OFTEN I HAVE PUSHED
MY FRIENDS
TO RUN FURTHER
TO RUN FASTER
TO SURPRISE THEMSELVES
WITH WHAT THEY
ACHIEVE
I STRUGGLE THOUGH
TO PUSH MYSELF
TO BREAK PAST
WHAT I'M DOING NOW
I NEED TO IMPROVE
IT'S NOT THE LEGS
IT'S NOT THE HEART
IT'S ALL IN THE MIND
I NEED MENTAL
STRENGTH

CELEBRATING HEALTHY MUMS

A LOT OF THE MUMS I FOLLOW ON TWITTER

ARE FOCUSED ON GETTING VERY MUCH FITTER

THEY RUN AND THEY SPIN AND LIFT HEAVY THINGS

NOT ONE OF THEM EVER A QUITTER

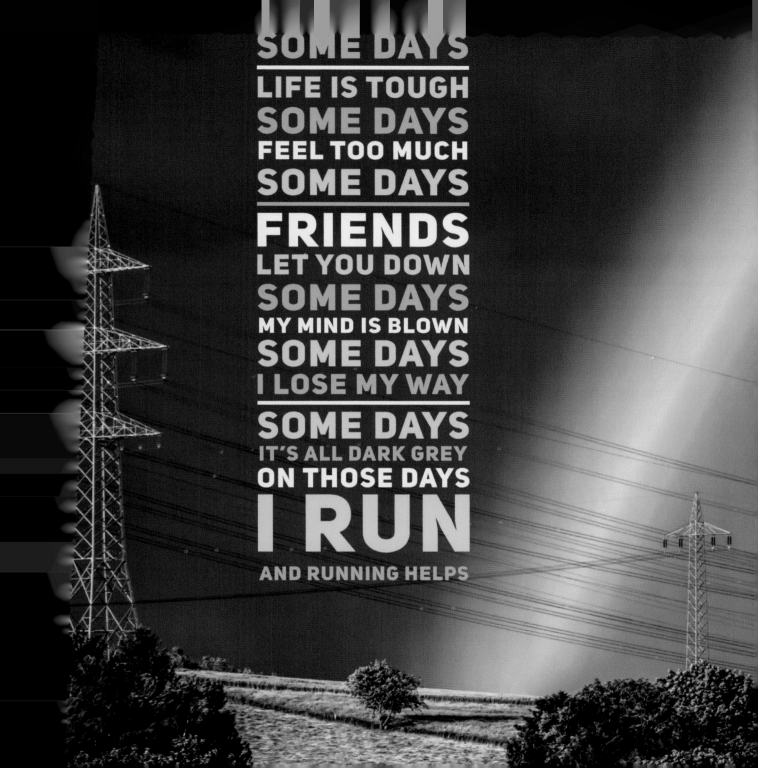

IT'S A NEW WEEK
YOUR CLEAN SLATE
YOUR FRESH PAGE
NO MENTION OF
SETBACKS
THE RUNS YOU
DIDN'T RUN
THE SESSIONS
THAT GOT MISSED
THE DAYS
THE SOFA WON
THIS WEEK YOU'LL
BE AMAZING
THIS WEEK
YOU WIN

ARE YOU READY?

LET'S GO RUNNING

I LOVE MY BODY

NOT BECAUSE IT'S GREAT

I'M PAST MY PRIME
A BIT OVERWEIGHT
BUT I RUN FOR MILES
NEVER THOUGHT I WOULD
OTHERS LOOK AT ME
AND WISH THEY COULD

THIS BODY HELPED
ME TO ACHIEVE
THINGS I SIMPLY
COULD NOT CONCEIVE

RUNNERS

AMAZE THEMSELVES
WITH WHAT THEY DO
SO I HOPE YOU LOVE
YOUR BODY TOO

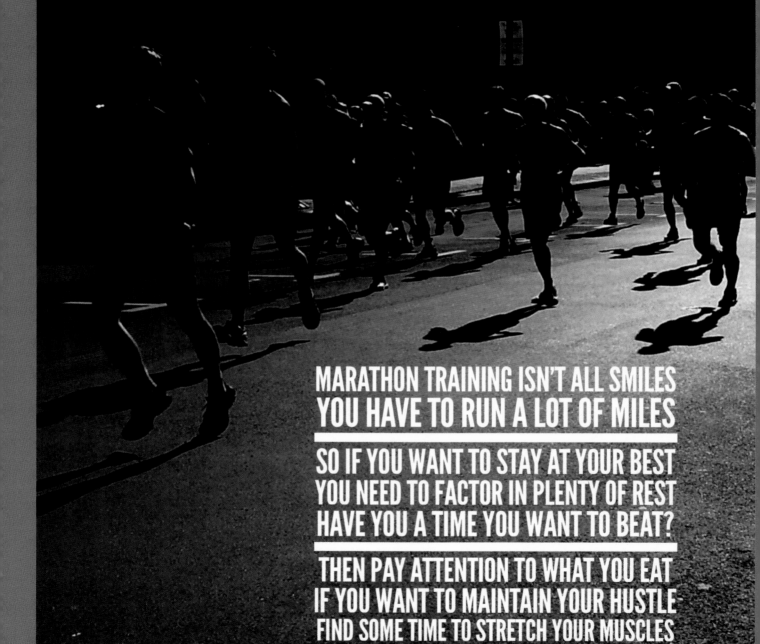

MARATHON TRAINING ISN'T ALL SMILES
YOU HAVE TO RUN A LOT OF MILES

SO IF YOU WANT TO STAY AT YOUR BEST
YOU NEED TO FACTOR IN PLENTY OF REST
HAVE YOU A TIME YOU WANT TO BEAT?

THEN PAY ATTENTION TO WHAT YOU EAT
IF YOU WANT TO MAINTAIN YOUR HUSTLE
FIND SOME TIME TO STRETCH YOUR MUSCLES

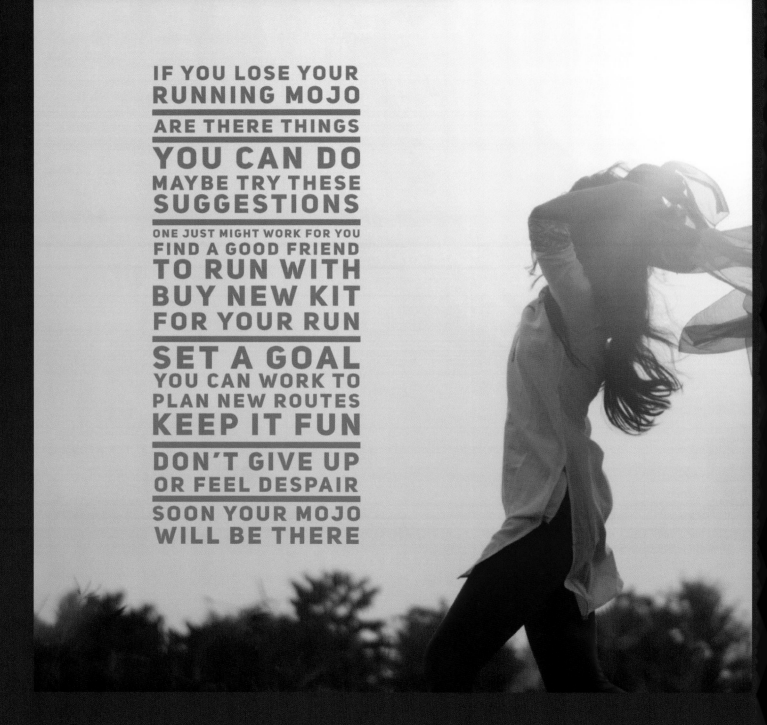

THE WORLD
SITS AND WAITS
SITS AND WATCHES TV
SITS AND SCROLLS
SITS AND SWIPES
SITS AND READS
A BIT OF THIS
A BIT OF THAT
SITS AND WISHES
WHILE THEY SIT
WE RUN
THE WIND
IN OUR HAIR
THE SUN
ON OUR CHEEKS
JOY IN OUR
HEARTS
CHOOSE MORE
STOP SCROLLING
START RUNNING

SOME OF MY FAVOURITE RUNNERS
DON'T RUN VERY FAR
BUT WILL ALWAYS GO
THE EXTRA MILE FOR OTHERS
THEY'RE NOT VERY FAST
BUT ARE ALWAYS QUICK

WITH A KIND WORD
STRUGGLE WITH ANXIETIES
BUT ARE ALWAYS THOUGHTFUL

MAY NOT HAVE MATCHING KIT
BUT ALWAYS WEAR A SMILE

THEY MIGHT NOT BE ELITE
BUT THEY HAVE TRUE CLASS

RUNNERS HAVE
BAD DAYS
TIMES WHEN IT'S TOUGH
LEGS FEEL LIKE STOPPING
YOUR MIND'S HAD ENOUGH
RUNNING'S
A FEELING
IT'S HAVING SOME HEART
TO KEEP YOURSELF GOING
IF YOU STRUGGLED TO START
SO DON'T GET FED UP
LET IT MESS WITH YOUR BRAIN
YOU'LL SOON BE RIGHT BACK
TO YOUR BEST
ONCE AGAIN

MANY OF MY
FAVOURITE RUNNERS
DON'T HAVE
AWESOME PACE
OFTEN AS THEY
RUN UP HILLS
THEY GO RED
IN THE FACE
BODY SHAPE IS
CUDDLY
MIND IS PRONE TO
DOUBTS
OFTEN IT'S A
BATTLE
FOR THEM TO GET OUT
YET THEY KEEP ON
RUNNING
CHEERING
ON OTHERS TOO
OUR COMMUNITY
IS RICHER
JUST BY HAVING YOU

YOU CALL YOURSELF
A RUNNER?
BUT YOU'RE SO SLOW
YOU NEED TO LOSE
SOME WEIGHT
YOUR KIT DOESN'T MATCH
YOU RUN SUCH
SHORT DISTANCES
YOU WALK
WHEN YOU GET TIRED
AND GET ALL
RED FACED
& SWEATY
SO WHAT SORT
OF RUNNER
ARE YOU?
MY SORT
YOU'RE A KEEPER
IF YOU RUN
YOU ARE A
REAL RUNNER!

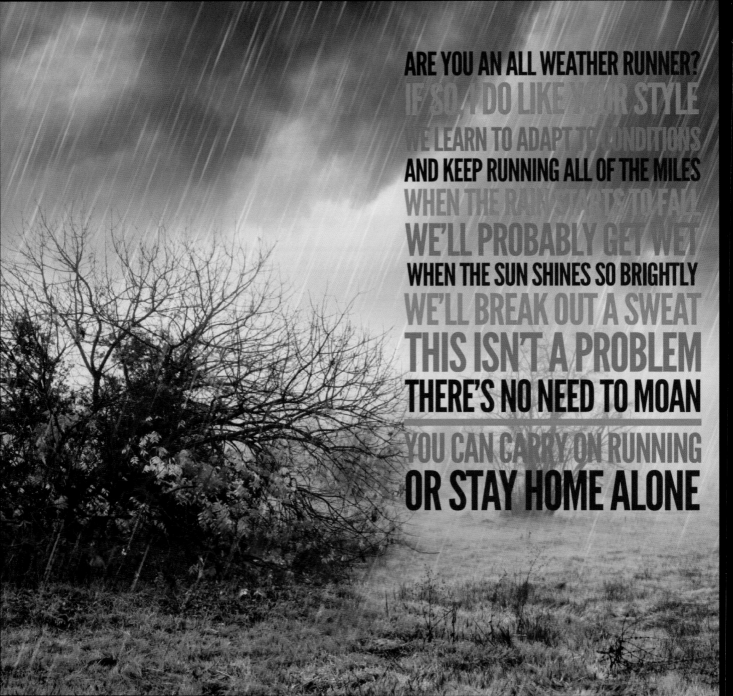

I RUN..

FOR PEACE OF MIND
TO KEEP FIT
TO LOSE A FEW POUNDS
FOR THE AMAZING FRIENDS

TO INSPIRE MY CHILDREN

FOR THE ENDORPHIN BUZZ
TO STAY HEALTHY
SO I CAN EAT CAKE
FOR OCCASIONAL BLING
TO HELP A CHARITY

FOR BETTER SLEEP
TO IMPROVE MENTAL HEALTH
BECAUSE I LOVE IT
WHY DO YOU RUN?
#KEEPRUNNING

THE JOY OF RUNNING IS
YOU CHOOSE!
YOU CHOOSE THE WHEN
AND THE WHERE
THE QUICK, THE SLOW
THE NEAR, THE FAR
THE FUN, THE CHALLENGE.
IT'S ALL AS INDIVIDUAL AS YOU.

BELIEVE

BELIEVE YOU'RE STRONG ENOUGH

BELIEVE YOU'RE FAST ENOUGH

BELIEVE YOU'RE GOOD ENOUGH

BELIEVE YOU CAN DO IT

BELIEVE IN YOU

DON'T EXPECT
PERFECTION
EVERY TIME YOU RUN
RUNNING
AS WITH LIFE
HAS GOOD DAYS AND BAD
DON'T PUSH HARD
EVERY TIME YOU RUN
SOMETIMES YOU NEED
TO RELAX AND
TAKE IT EASY
DON'T RUN FAST
EVERY TIME YOU RUN
YOU'LL END UP
FRUSTRATED
OR WORSE, INJURED
BUT WHEN IT ALL CLICKS
ENJOY THE MAGIC

IT DOESN'T MATTER
IF YOU'VE BEEN RUNNING
ONE DAY, OR TEN YEARS

IT DOESN'T MATTER
IF YOU RUN A MARATHON
OR A MILE IN THE PARK

IT DOESN'T MATTER
IF YOU CAN RUN
A FOUR MINUTE MILE
OR FOUR MILES IN AN HOUR
IF YOU RUN, YOU ARE A RUNNER
THERE ARE NO EXCEPTIONS
BE PROUD TO BE
A RUNNER

THAT'S A NICE
MEDAL
WHAT IS IT
MADE OF?

TEARS,
SWEAT
AND
DETERMINATION!